Manfred Intenthron

and

John Gerrard

MAKING NESTS

FOR

BUMBLE BEES

A way to save an endangered species

MAKING NESTS FOR BUMBLE BEES
© Manfred Intenthron and John Gerrard

All rights reserved. No part of this publication may be reproduced, stored in a retrieval system, transmitted in any form or by any means electronic, mechanical, including photocopying, recording or otherwise without prior consent of the copyright holders.

ISBN 978-0-86098-286-9

Originally published 1999

Reprinted 2003

This edition 2018

All rights reserved. No part of this publication may be reproduced, stored in a retrieval system, transmitted in any form or by any means electronic, mechanical, including photocopying, recording or otherwise without the prior consent of the copyright holder

Jointly published by
The International Bee Research Association
A Company limited by Guarantee,
91, Brinsea Road, Congresbury, Bristol BS49 5JJ (UK)

and

Northern Bee Books
Scout Bottom Farm, Mytholmroyd, Hebden Bridge HX7 5JS (UK)

Obtainable from:
www.ibrabee.org.uk
&
www.northernbeebooks.co.uk

Printed by Lightning Source, UK

Manfred Intenthron

and

John Gerrard

MAKING NESTS

FOR

BUMBLE BEES

A way to save an endangered species

CONTENTS

Chapters		Page Nos.
1.	Introduction	1
2.	The life and times of Bumble Bees	3
3.	Nest Boxes	7
4.	The Nest	3
5.	Feeding the bees in the nest	5
6.	Successful nests and introducing queens into nests	17
7.	After-care, pests and parasites	21
	Practical Nest Box Designs	24

FURTHER READING

Alford, D.V. (1978) *The life of the Bumble Bee*. Davis Poynter, London.

Chinery, Michael (1976) *Insects of Britain and Northern Europe*. Collins, London.

Gibbons, Bob (1995) *Field Guide to Insects of Britain and Northern Europe*. The Crowood Press, Marlborough.

IBRA (1996) *Bumble Bees for Pleasure and Profit*. IBRA, Cardiff.

Prys-Jones, O.E. & Corbet, S.A. (1991) *Bumblebees*. The Richmond Publishing Co. Ltd, Slough.

Sladen, F.W.L. (1989) *The Humble-bee, its Life History and how to Domesticate it*. Logaston Press., Hereford.
Available from www.northernbeebooks.co.uk

The inspiration behind this book is Manfred Intenthron who has been fascinated by bumble bees since he was 6 years old. He loves them and what he knows about them comes from his own observations and not from books. When two years ago I gave him the book by F.W.L. Sladen to read he said: " What more is there to say? It's all here." But that is not true. There is still a lot more to say and he knows some of it as this book shows.

Thirty years ago Manfred and his family moved to a suburban house with a back garden. It is about $1/2$ mile (1 km) from the centre of a town with a population of 70,000 and the garden measures about 900 sq. yards. (750 sq. metre), a very ordinary size. Gradually Manfred planted it with flowers to attract his bumble bees and then started to experiment with artificial nests to keep them there. He has now learned the art and for the last 5 years his garden has been home to about 30 nests each year, an extraordinary achievement.

Manfred is now 72 years old but still spends the winter getting his home-made bumble bee nests ready, the spring making sure they are occupied and the summer looking after the growing colonies inside them. He says he still has a lot to learn.

John Gerrard

Worcestershire, England 1999

CHAPTER 1
INTRODUCTION

Insects are generally seen as unfriendly things. Wasps are aggressive and sting us painfully. Flies are dirty and settle on our food. The sly mosquito bites us in the night. But bumble bees are different. They are furry and soft and warm. They are never a nuisance. They just bumble around among the flowers making that lovely deep buzz which is the sound of summer. They only sting when they need to defend themselves which happens rarely. Along with butterflies and grasshoppers, they are considered nice insects.

Bumble bees are also very valuable to man because of what they do for farmers. Like bees they collect pollen and in so doing pollinate many flowers. The bumble bees that have long tongues are among the few insects that can pollinate certain crops such as field beans. In fact some wild flowers depend on them for their survival. Unlike bumble bees, other insects leave these flowers alone because they cannot reach deep enough inside them to suck up the nectar.

Suddenly bumble bees have become an endangered species. Their traditional feeding ground is a pasture full of flowers like clover. Their nests are found in the wild and neglected bits of land like the hedgerows and the unploughed and ungrazed margins of fields – all those untidy patches that used to abound round the farms of the past. Now this wild side of farming is disappearing, sacrificed because it is not efficient enough, not productive enough. Hedgerows are ripped out to make fields larger. Field margins are reduced as far as possible. The inorganic fertilisers that are used to increase yields discourage the growth of flowering plants – except for things like nettles and docks. Herbicides are sprayed with the aim of killing flowering plants because these are the weeds in the non-flowering corn. Pesticides are indiscriminate and kill or weaken bumble bees as well as aphids. It is no wonder that in areas like East Anglia there are now few bumble bees to be seen.

Many people are now thinking that our wildlife is an asset that must be preserved and there is a move towards environmentally friendly farming. However the Common Agricultural Policy, the view that a farm is a factory for the production of food and the need for farmers to make a decent living are all factors pulling in the other direction. Bumble bees will probably become very rare if their survival depends on a change in farming practice. Even if that did eventually come about it might be too late.

If the bumble bee is to flourish, one place that can become its haven is the garden. Flowers, which are their food supply, are what every gardener grows. All gardeners aim to have flowers all the year round and in great variety which is what bumble bees, and lots of other insects, need before anything else. However bumble bees must also produce the next generation if they are to survive and what they seek as nest sites are not what the average gardener would consider to be "neat and tidy". Bumble bees are like old mouse nests, holes in the ground, clumps of dead grass and untidy hedge bottoms. They are also fussy about what will make a good nest. Any old hole will not do.

In this book we show gardeners and others how to provide a bumble bee with a suitable home in a garden or elsewhere, even if they have already ruined several sites by tidying up.

CHAPTER 2
THE LIFE AND TIMES OF BUMBLE BEES

While this book is about making and setting up man-made nests that will be attractive to bumble bees, it is important that you know the basic facts of their life history. This will be a very short account but if you wish to know more there is a suggested reading list at the front.

The fertile bumble bee queen emerges from hibernation in the spring, usually during March or April. Because her winter reserves of fat are exhausted she immediately starts to build up her strength by feeding on the nectar and pollen in spring flowers. When she is fully fit, she will start to search for a suitable nest site. Once she has found one to her liking, she occupies it and makes it into her nest. This she does by arranging the nest materials already in the site to make a warm chamber with a soft but firm base for the next stage. She will never fetch materials from outside the nest to add to those already there. When the nest is ready, she constructs two "cells". These are untidy little pots made of wax and pollen with a lump of pollen at the bottom. In one she lays the first batch of eggs. The other she fills with nectar. She then "broods" the eggs, keeping them warm with her body and feeding on the nectar.

The eggs hatch into larvae and the queen then forages to keep them supplied with pollen and nectar. The larvae grow quickly because she keeps them warm. When they pupate, she will construct new cells alongside the first ones and lay another batch of eggs.

It takes about 5 weeks from an egg being laid to the emergence of an adult bumble bee from the pupa. The first eggs hatch into worker bees which are smaller versions of the queen herself and which immediately start to help her by foraging and doing "housework". As the colony develops and the number of workers grows, the queen spends less time foraging and more time laying eggs and caring for the larvae.

Later in the summer, when the colony has reached its peak, the queen lays her last batches of eggs which this time develop into males and queens. These new adults forage only for themselves and never play any part in looking after the parental nest, although the new queens may return to the nest at night. By day, the males patrol their own particular flight paths and leave scent markers at key points to attract the queens. Most queens, but not all, mate but all will spend the rest of the summer building up reserves of fat and honey in their body for the winter to come. In the autumn they find a place to hibernate, usually by making a small dry cavity underground, where they remain until the next spring. The nest where they were reared is by now abandoned and the old queen, her workers and the males will not survive the winter.

There are relatively few animals that rear their young after they hatch from the egg. In this early stage of life all animals are very vulnerable to predators, bad weather and a shortage of food. To have an adult devoted to protecting them and feeding them gives them a much greater chance of survival. One common way of protecting the young is to set them in a nest and all nests have features that are the same whatever the animal.

Firstly, nests are placed so that they cannot be seen and will provide some natural protection. Mammals often choose a chamber underground and birds often choose trees.

Secondly, nests must be kept dry, which means protection from rain and good drainage to allow water to escape. It also means that there must be good ventilation, not only to provide the fresh air that is needed for healthy development but also to dry any bedding that is damp as a result of condensation, excretion etc. Growing animals lose a lot of water from their bodies.

Thirdly, nests must be warm otherwise growth will be slow. The centre of a thriving bumble bee nest will be over 30°C, which is almost blood heat. Nests, therefore, need to be well insulated by warm bedding.

Finally, the nest must be kept clean and there may be a need for a "latrine" area nearby. As an example of these four requirements, take an underground "mouse" nest. It is well protected. The nest chamber will be higher than surrounding passages to allow drainage. The earth surrounding the nest may seem damp but it is a very good absorbent of moisture. There will be several entrances, which are not just escape routes but also ventilation ducts and somewhere to put rubbish. The nest itself will be a ball of fine dry grass laid carefully for breathable warmth.

Bumble bees have nests that follow all the same rules. The difference between them and other animals is that they do not make their own nests. Instead they take over the abandoned nest of another animal, e.g. a mouse or a bird. They choose it carefully and then adapt it to suit their own use.

Bumble bees are exclusively vegetarian, living on pollen and nectar which can, of course, only be found in flowers. Nectar is the carbohydrate or energy giving part of the diet but is not produced by all flowers. It is collected by the long tongue which bumble bees can use to reach deep into a long tubular flower. Pollen is the protein part which can be found in all flowers even though bees only visit some of them. It is collected on the hairs and bristles of their body and then placed in "baskets" on their hind legs. Without enough suitable flowers within reasonable flying distance of their nests, say a half mile at the very most, bumble bees and honey bees cannot survive. There is, therefore, no point in providing nests for them if there are not enough flowers close by.

There are six species of bumble bee, all of the genus *Bombus*, that are common throughout England and Wales and another 16 or so that are uncommon or rare. (No species is really common in Scotland or Ireland.) To be able to identify them properly one needs pictures and better descriptions than those that follow.

The six common species are:
B. terrestris: This is dark with two brownish yellow stripes and a brownish white or buff coloured tail. It is the first to emerge in the spring, usually March, and makes a large colony, always underground and reached by a tunnel, which it likes to be long.
B. lucorum: A fat bee with two bright yellow stripes and a white tail which also emerges early. It also makes large nests and prefers them underground but without such a long tunnel.
B. lapidarius: A big black bee with an orange tail which emerges about a month later. Its nests are large and underground like B. terrestris.
B. hortorum: A dark bumble bee with yellow bands and a white tail. Queens are late to emerge and make smallish nests above ground. They have very long tongues and are the best species for pollinating beans and clover.
B. pascuorum: A completely ginger bumble bee with variable stripes on its abdomen which emerges late, say May. It likes to feed on long tubular flowers. It makes a smallish nest above ground. This is a "carder" bee because it combs nest material to cover the cells in the nest.

B. pratorum: A small agile black bee with yellow bands and an orange tail, it commonly visits flowers that hang downwards. It makes its nests above or below ground but the colonies are usually small and have a short season.

All animals and plants suffer because they are considered a source of food or shelter or both by other living things. Bumble bees are no exception. There is one serious pest of their nests two serious parasites.

The pest is the black ant (not the red ant). Ants are always on the look-out for food. If one ant discovers the way into a bumble bee's nest and then the ready supply there of nectar and pollen used to feed the growing larvae, it will quickly "tell" all the others in its own nest. Soon a procession of ants will arrive and they will strip the nest bare and so destroy it.

The first parasite is the cuckoo bee of the genus *Psithyrus*. In fact there are several species of cuckoo bumble bees each of which is a parasite of the one particular species of bumble bee which it resembles. The queen cuckoo bee, which emerges from hibernation late, invades the nest of the host bee and lays her own eggs there to be looked after by the host workers. She often destroys host larvae and may kill the host queen. The cuckoo larvae develop into either queens or males, never workers. When they leave the nest, they mate and the new queens then feed and hibernate like true bumble bees.

The other serious parasite is the wax moth, which also parasitises bee hives. This oblong undistinguished-looking grey moth invades in summer when the nest is well established. Inside, it lays its eggs which soon hatch into pale larvae which may first be seen on the nest material. As the larvae develop they spin a fibrous web around themselves and invade the larval cells, eating every thing as they go. They quickly destroy the whole colony and then move to a sheltered place, perhaps within the nest area, where they spin a strong fibrous cocoon. Here they spend the winter. In spring they pupate and then emerge as moths in the following summer.

There are other pests that affect bumble bees, such as mites, but they do not generally prevent the development of the colony and the emergence of a new generation of fertile queens.

CHAPTER 3
NEST BOXES

There are two parts to an artificial bumble bee nest, the nest box and the nest inside the nest box. Here we describe the features of the nest box.

The first thing to say is that there is fundamentally no need for a nest box at all. A bumble bee wants a nest and is not interested in its container. In fact many natural nests are found in tussocks of grass and have no hard boundaries. However in practice an artificial nest must be placed in a container so that it can be manufactured away from its ultimate site, moved when necessary, inspected during the season and cleaned at the end of it ready fro next year. The longer it lasts the better.

The second thing to say is that only one design of nest box is theoretically needed even though some bumble bees prefer nests above ground and some below, some with the entrance directly into the nest and some approached by a tunnel. A searching queen will accept anything that meets her true needs. Any material can be used; for example wood – plywood is easily formed into a box but wood seems to attract the wax moth; plastic – one flower pot can make the roof and sides, two can make the complete box; metal – an old paint tin is durable and can be adapted; or concrete – two castings, a base and a lid, make something that will last for years and years. Always remember that you will want easy access to the inside.

The nest box should be designed as follows:

Internal Dimensions

Minimum 150x150x150 mm (6x6x6 inches) for small surface nests. Maximum 250x250x250 mm (8x8x8 inches) for large nests above or below ground.

Sometimes if you are lucky, the nest develops into one that is very strong with up to 400 bees at different stages of development. In this case you will want to expand the nest so it is worth considering a design which allows for this rather rare event.

Shape

Because the nest box has to house not only the nest but also a feeder and a latrine area, it is an advantage if it is a little longer than it is wide so there is space away from the round nest.

Number Of Chambers

There is no need for more than one chamber in the nest. Some designs recommend two but this does not happen in nature. However it is essential that there is space around the actual nest within the nest box, firstly to provide ventilation but secondly to leave room for the latrine area and the feeder. (See Chapter 5)

Ventilation

This is a key requirement of a successful nest, especially as the container will probably be made of a material which does not absorb moisture and may even encourage condensation. The nest must never be allowed to get damp.

Apart from any entrance, there should be a minimum of two ventilation holes about 40mm (1.5 inches) diameter but preferably more. Within reason, the more holes there are the better. Holes should be placed so that there is a flow of air through the nest, i.e. from bottom to top and from side to side. Nests actually buried in the ground will need a 40mm ventilation pipe taking the air beneath the nest and up through the drainage hole. (See below.) It will also certainly need ventilation "chimneys" leading from the top.

To prevent ants and other pests getting into the nest, ventilation holes must be covered with a durable fine mesh net, e.g. polyester net curtain material or wire gauze, especially in the early stages. This applies to all holes apart from entrances and drainage holes which cannot be reached from the surface. Later, when the nest is well established, there is not so much danger from unprotected holes.

Protection from rain

Any holes that could let rain into the nest box and dampen the nest itself should be shielded in some way, e.g. by a lid that overhangs the sides of the box.

Drainage

There should be some way for the water that does get into the nest to drain away. Ideally the bottom of the box should slope to a drainage hole which leads directly into the ground and is covered with wire mesh to support the nest and allow air to circulate underneath it.

Light

The nest should be kept relatively dark.

OUTSIDE APPEARANCE

The bees do not care! However they do have strong views about the entrance.

Inside Finish

Take care that there is nothing that can poison the bees who touch the inside surface. Remember what the container was used for in the past.

Entrances

Different bumble bees have differing preferences for the site of their nest and the type of entrance to it. Some look for an "underground" nest which obviously needs an "underground" passage leading to it. Those that naturally nest on the surface may look for one with several entrances or one with a surface passage leading to it. For some guidance on what to provide for a particular species, refer to the description of the six common species in the previous chapter.

Entrances should be based on the following guidelines:

Internal Diameter

A hole of diameter 20 to 40 mm (0.75 to 1.5 inches). Some bees, e.g. *B. pascuorum*, tolerate a much wider and "looser" entrance. Also bees searching for a nest are attracted by a hole that is clearly visible, i.e. large, even if it narrows to something much smaller further in.

Position

In the early stages and excepting tunnels, an entrance should be on a level with the ground because this is where the bees look for it. To make it more obvious, the earth can be marked with scratches leading to it as if it had been used by a mouse. Bees seldom look for a nest above ground. Later, when the nest is established, the entrance can be altered so that it is not at ground level in order to discourage ants, e.g. by removing some of the earth from around it.

Tunnels

These should be the same diameter as entrances and made of rigid tubing, e.g. 22mm (0.9 inches) plastic piping. Lengths can be from a few cms. (inches) to a metre (yard) depending on the species of bumble bee. If water can get in through the entrance it must be able to drain away before it reaches the nest, e.g. through strategically placed holes. Tunnels do not need to run deep in the ground. Bees can be easily fooled by covering the tube with turf.

There is danger that snails, which generally feed at night, will use the entrance to a tunnel as a convenient day-time resting place. When they do they will block the one way in and out of the nest during daylight and so cause the death of the colony. To prevent this, drill a small hole in the top and bottom of the tubing close to the entrance and thread a piece of wire or a nail through. The result is a narrower entrance but it will still be big enough for the bees.

Lining The Nest Box

Because ventilation is so important, place something like wire netting round the inside of the nest box to keep the neat away from the sides and underneath the nest to raise it above the floor. For example, a wire "basket" could be made to contain the nest itself provided it does not restrict its size too much. A lining also allows space for the latrine and somewhere to place the feeder.

An Underground Nest

As intimated above, it is easy to fool a queen bumble bee that to think she has found an underground nest even though it is nothing of the sort. All that is needed is an "underground" passage leading into a dark nest. Sink the nest box a few centimetres (inches) into the ground and run a tube just below the surface to an entrance which has the earth built up above it to make a very small bank. In this way, ventilation and access are little different to a surface nest and easy to arrange but to the bees it is an underground nest.

Disguising The Nest Box

It is probably unnecessary to disguise the nest box but it is certainly very important to make the entrance, whether on the surface or at the start of a long tunnel, look as natural as possible. (For details of how to do this see "Attracting queens" in Chapter 6) However, if the entrance is a hole in the side of the nest box it is wise to disguise the box. An easy way is to smear glue over the lower part of the box and stick dried vegetation to it, e.g. bracken or moss. This breaks up the regular shape of the box.

CHAPTER 4
THE NEST

The actual nest, so long as it is kept dry and free of predators, is the key to attracting bumble bees to a nest site. They have been known to nest in a sack of old hay hung up in a barn or the contents of a vacuum cleaner bag left in an abandoned dust-bin, which gives a clue to what they like.

The main purpose of the nest is to maintain the right environment for the developing colony started by the queen. This means keeping it warm because where it is placed already keeps it dry. The optimum temperature for the development of the larvae is about 30°C (85°F) and when necessary bumble bees tending a colony will generate heat by vibrating their wings in order to reach this level. On cold days this can take a long time. Therefore, insulation to prevent heat being lost is very important. At the same time the nest should not become too hot. The location of the nest and plenty of ventilation are the best safeguards.

In nature insulation means that the queen must find inside the nest site a ball of fine fibres which she can work into the nest she needs. Lack of enough fibres of the right sort will cause her to reject the nest, however good the site that contains it, because she can never add to what is there. In fact, the quality and quantity of the nest materials are crucial to attracting a queen to the nest.

Materials

To provide good insulation, fibres must be fine. To give shape to the nest, they must be long enough and stiff enough. Fibres that will tangle together are an advantage. In practice it is easier to use a combination of different fibres to get the desired result and anything can be used provided it will not harm the bees. The chief danger is the use of tough synthetic fibres like nylon and polyester. A bee that becomes tangled with a natural fibre like cotton can chew through it but it cannot cope with synthetic fibres and will probably die.

A good combination of natural fibres is **moss** and **upholsterers' padding**. Moss must be of a fine texture, absolutely dry and without dust and dirt. You can usually find something suitable in a deciduous wood. Gather sufficient and then spread it out to dry in a warm place. Upholsterers' padding can be obtained form upholsterers! Choose the stuff that comes out of old chairs or mattresses because it usually consists of natural fibres only. New material nearly always contains synthetic fibres. Open it out like the moss.

Alternatively you can buy suitable materials. For the fine fibres choose **kapok**, a natural vegetable material which is very soft. To stiffen it, buy from a pet shop **hamster bedding** made form well-shredded cellulose,.

To make a nest you will need to mix four parts of **cotton** or **kapok** with one of **moss** or **hamster bedding**. Make sure the mix is even and is well fluffed up to provide the best insulation.

Although it gets dirty and damp during use, this material can be used for several years provided it is cleaned each year. An easy way to clean it is to pass it through a garden shredder which will not only get rid of the dust and dirt but also fluff it up to make it attractive to bees.

There is one other valuable material, namely old mouse nests. Do not use it for making nests but as an attraction for the queens as we describe in Chapter 6.

Making The Nest In The Nest Box

Open up the nest box and lay a platform of **moss** (or **hamster bedding**) on the wire netting platform in the bottom. This coarse material traps a layer of air under the nest proper. Now with both hands gather up a good bundle of the mixed material, shape it into a ball and place it on the platform of moss. Make sure there is space round the sides for ventilation. Poke a hole in the ball with your finger opposite the entrance to attract the queen inside. It does not need to be elaborate because she will always move and arrange the material where and how she wants it.

CHAPTER 5
FEEDING THE BEES IN THE NEST

Providing the nest is attractive, a queen bumble bee will occupy it and start to rear the next generation without any further help. However, an artificial food source within the nest is an advantage in the early stages for two reasons. The first is that the queen is often under-nourished when she comes out of hibernation and flowers may be scarce. If there is food already in the nest she inspects, she will not only find it more attractive but also be able to rest there and build up her strength. This is particularly true in bad weather, i.e. when it is cold or wet or both, because she cannot go out to look for food and has not yet built up any stores in the nest. As a result we can prevent a nest from failure. The second reason is that it is very necessary when introducing queens into a nest artificially, which is the subject of a later chapter.

Feeder

This is the container for the **feed**. It should hold enough to last a few days, be easy to fill, place within the nest and refill; be easy for the bees to feed from without getting in a mess; and be protected from the nest which might fall into it.

An example is a simple "dish" covered with some sort of open-meshed fabric. The dish can be the plastic screw top off any container provided that it is the right size, i.e. something between 25mm and 40mm (1 and 1½ inches) in diameter and 10mm to 15mm (½ inch) deep. This is covered by a disc of open fabric made from synthetic fibres, for example nylon net or the stuff which makes a bag that holds oranges in a supermarket. The fabric for this platform should not be too open because the bees will be walking on it but open enough to allow them to feed through it. The disc should be cut a little larger than the diameter of the "dish".

For version 1, which is used where the nest material might smother the feeder (e.g. Nest Box Design 2) sandpaper the rim of the dish, run a bead of strong proprietary glue round the rim and press it onto the disc of net. When dry, trim the net. Now fit an "umbrella" which is simply a piece of plastic cut from something like a margarine container. Cut it so that a round piece from the bottom of the container forms the umbrella and a strip from the side connected to it forms the support. The support is then tucked into an elastic band fitted round the feeder. The feed is poured into the dish through the net.

For Version 2, which is used where the feeder is placed into the nest box through holes, e.g. Nest Box Design 1, drill a small hole in the top edge of the feeder and tie a piece of thin twine to it leaving a tail of at least 100mm (4inches). Now stick the net to the rim as in Version 1.

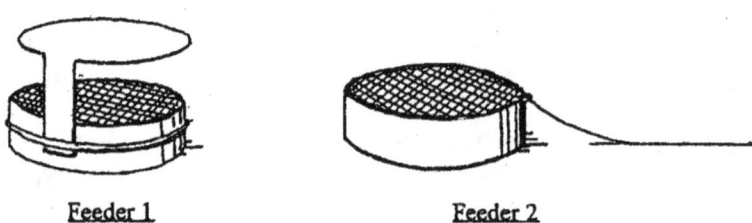

Feeder 1   Feeder 2

The feed itself is simple to make. It consists of a strong mixture of sugar and water – or honey and water if you prefer. The proportions are not critical but about 1 teaspoon of sugar to 1 tablespoon of water or equal volumes of honey and water are about right. Put enough in the dish so that not only will it last for some time but also the bees can reach it with their tongues. Bumble bees can cope with a distance of up to 1 cm (½ inch) between the platform and the liquid.

CHAPTER 6
SUCCESSFUL NESTS AND INTRODUCING QUEENS INTO NESTS

Placing A Nest Box

It is important that you have your nest box ready in the Spring. Place it outside early in March where you hope it will attract a searching queen. The queens of some species will probably still be searching at the end of April and into May but others come out of hibernation much earlier.

The nest should be set reasonably level and must be secure. Hide it in a bank or hedge bottom if you can because queens tend to look there. Avoid places where it will be scorched by the sun or buffeted by the wind. Make sure it is not an eyesore. If it is where it can be seen from your house it makes not only for easy checking but also for much entertainment when the nest is working.

Attracting Queens

Even if your nest is five star it will never be occupied if queens fail to examine it. Holes that invite investigation are essential. Queens look for something natural and well-established; the mouse nest they search is last year's model, not freshly made. Therefore put old vegetation or rocks round the hole and shape it to make it appear wll used. Scratch the ground to make a path like a mouse run leading to the hole, especially if it is tunnel.

The other thing to do is of more uncertain provenance. It is believed that queens are attracted by the scent of mice. Therefore, find someone with pet mice, e.g. a pet shop, and ask them to give you some old mouse bedding which you can place in the nest and by the entrance and also some mouse droppings which you can drop by the entrance.

Successful Nests

Hopefully you will be lucky and a queen bumble bee will occupy your nest naturally but often you will be unlucky. You can check to see whether the nest is occupied as follows. In the evening, when the queen and any workers are always at home, tap the outside of the box increasingly hard with a stick to make a noise. If there are bees inside they will make a deep and angry humming for several seconds.

If you have been lucky, there is little that you can do for the time being except fill the feeder. Do this in the evening when you will disturb the colony least and using a torch that is not too bright. The real danger to the colony now is that ants will discover it and the few bees present will be too weak to provide an adequate defence. (See Chapter 7.) Later, when the colony is well established, have a look inside. On a fine day, take off the top of the box, move the nest material to one side and look at its organisation, the cells with larvae inside and the busy workers. Try to leave the nest as you found it. By this stage there will be no need for a feeder.

When you open the nest, some of the bees may fly out through this opening instead of the proper one. Do not worry. Leave the lid open until they go back inside and then shut it. Once inside they will find the usual way out.

Introducing Queens

Bumble bees can be infuriating. They will fly past your beautiful nest without even noticing it. They may even go inside and apparently reject it without really looking at it. It is therefore a very good idea to introduce a queen into it by force and try to persuade her to stay. Here is how to do it.

Catching And Transporting

Before catching a queen you must be sure that she has not already got a nest. The best sign is that she is obviously looking for one, flying close to the ground, landing, going down likely holes. If you catch one that is feeding, make sure she is not carrying pollen which is a sure sign that she has a nest already.

Bumble bees, best of all, are remarkably easy to catch compared to a lot of insects. The time and the place to catch them is when they are looking for a nest site or failing that when they are feeding in or on a flower. Remember, they seldom sting! When they are searching, catch them under an open jam jar or transparent plastic pot as they investigate the ground. On a flower, catch them in a small container with a wide mouth and a secure top; we find the little cylinders that are used as packs for 35mm film or transparent music cassette tape cases ideal. If the container is airtight you must make several holes in it to let in air if you use it as a temporary carrier. Bees are quieter when kept in the dark and will seldom come to any harm on a short journey but do not put two in the same pot. If the journey will be a long one, put each in a temporary nest box as described next.

When you arrive home you should introduce each bee straight away into either a nest or a temporary nest box. This latter is small, e.g. a margarine carton. It must be secure and well ventilated and should contain a small amount of nest material and a feeder. Use a skewer to bodge holes in the sides for ventilation. To get the bee inside, you will need to cut a small trapdoor in the lid; make sure it will not spring open after shutting. It is also an advantage to put a window in the lid too so that you can monitor the mood of the bee; cut a hole and cover it with transparent plastic which is stuck in place with an all purpose adhesive. There is an easy way to move a bee between different containers. First release it by a closed window – without other open windows nearby. The bee will fly to the window. This is a good time to examine and identify it. Now cover it with a small catching pot and slide a piece of card between the container and the glass. Carry the container and card like this to the new home, place its mouth over the entrance and slide the card away.

Introducing A Queen Into A Nest

There is no point introducing a queen into a nest until and unless she is lively. Keep her in the temporary home until she is rested and revived. The signs are restlessness, occasional buzzing and a constant search for a way out.

Choose the best type of nest box for the particular species you have caught. There is no point putting an underground nester in a surface nest because she will not stay. If it has been standing outside, make sure there is not a queen in there already. Prepare the nest and insert a full feeder. Block off all the entrances bar one with anything suitable. Remember that the blockers must stay in place for 2 days. Have the blocker for the last hole at hand. Now introduce the queen into the nest, keeping the container pressed tightly against the opening until you are sure the bee is inside. Quickly remove the container, checking the bee is not still inside it, and block up this last hole.

Leave the nest undisturbed for 48 hours; the queen will not suffer. Hopefully she will find the nest attractive. Open <u>one hole</u>. Now it is a matter of watching and waiting and checking for continued occupation.

Queens that are introduced like this do not always take to the nest. Perhaps they do not like it. Perhaps they have a nest already – they will always return home. Or perhaps they are sterile. Quite a lot of queens never mate successfully but still hibernate and look for nests in the Spring, which is rather sad.

Chapter 7
After Care, Pests And Parasites

After Care

As pointed out in the last chapter, there is little that needs to be done to a successful nest except to check on its health and to look for pests and parasites. The general danger is damp; there must always be good drainage and plenty of ventilation. Sometimes a nest will be very successful and become cramped for space. Add more nest material if you can but often you need to make extra room too which may be impossible.

To make it more difficult for the parasites, camouflage the entrance by making it appear smaller, for example by putting moss round it. Always do this at night when the bees are all in the nest. They will not be able to recognise the new entrance until they have full reconnoitred around it when they emerge in the morning. Later, the bees will arrange things as want them.

Pests and Parasites

Black Ants

These are without doubt a serious pest. If they find a nest, which contains the attraction of pots of honey, pollen and small grubs, they will come in their hundreds until it is quite destroyed. The bees in the nest will do their best to defend it when it is in the early stages of development they can be easily overwhelmed.

The best defence is to prevent the first ant finding the nest. Try to place the bees' nest far away from ant nests. Obstruct all ventilation holes and entrances, except the one in use with ant-proof fabric such as polyester net of a fine mesh, e.g. net curtaining, or plastic foam. Block up every hole that is large enough for an ant to get through. If it is possible, lengthen the main entrance on the outside with a piece of tubing that is above ground level; the bees will quickly get used to it. The middle section of this tubing can be coated <u>outside</u> with a ring of bird-lime or insecticide to make an even stronger deterrent. Be careful with insecticide it kills bees as well as ants.

Another ploy is to provide the ants with diversions. A jar full of sugar and water that is sunk in the ground can catch lots. They fall in and cannot get out. Alternatively it may be possible to destroy, or at least weaken, the ant nest.

If all this fails there may be nothing that can be done; the nest is doomed. However it is worth trying to move the whole nest complete to a new site if things have not gone too far. Do it at night with the entrance blocked. The bees inside will soon come to terms with their new surroundings. Some bees may not have made it back to the nest before dark so leave a little nest material where the old nest was placed. The next night you can scoop this up with the bees inside and put them in their proper home.

Cuckoo Bees (Psithyrus)

It is very hard to prevent a Cuckoo Bee finding a nest because it is part of their nature. Once inside it will use its superior strength to overwhelm and usually kill the queen. It will then take over the nest, using the existing workers to rear the eggs it lays in the pots. By this stage there is nothing that can be done – except observe what is happening and marvel at nature.

The only hope of preserving the bumble bees is to prevent the cuckoo bee finding the nest or to catch it before it gets to work. This latter ploy means constant observation – and, of course, the ability to tell the difference between a bumble bee and a cuckoo bee. They are very good mimics. If you do find one before things have gone too far. The only hope is to kill it – or at least to transport it well away from your nest.

The Wax Moth

This is another serious pest which attacks honey bees as well as bumble bees. Again, the best method of defence is to prevent it getting into the nest but, again, it is hard to stop once the nest has been discovered. You can try to remove the eggs or grubs if things have not gone too far but that is easier said than done. Perhaps you should just watch life as it is – "red in tooth and claw".

Other Things To Do

Records

Records are always interesting when you look at them later on and can be very useful. Bumble bees are becoming increasingly rare so your sittings and experiences might be invaluable. As a start, record the number of nests you put out, what type they were and the number that were occupied; what species you saw and which were attracted to your nests; the size of each nest at its height and problems you encountered, especially with pests and parasites.

End Of Season Work

Between the end of one season and the start of the next, the old nests need to be cleaned out. Empty out the old nest material and wash and dry the nest box. Make sure the drainage and ventilation systems are still good. Do any running repairs or modifications that are needed.

Now sort out the old nest material, only keeping that which is in good condition even if it is a bit dirty and matted. Shred this old material, either by hand or in a garden shredder, until it is again fluffy, clean and open. Leave it spread out in the air but protected form the rain until it regains its freshness. In these circumstances, any vermin left in it will either go elsewhere or die off.

You now have the boxes and most of the materials you need to start the new season. With the experience of the last, you will surely do better this time………

PRACTICAL NEST BOX DESIGNS

The designs that follow are all based on materials that can be readily bought in shops or garden centres. However there is no need to follow them slavishly. Use whatever you have to hand and modify them accordingly.

Nest Box Design 1

This is a large nest box that will cater for every type of bumble bee and also for large colonies. It has a choice of four entrances, one of which can be made into a tunnel by fitting a piece of plastic tubing into its mouth. As explained, if it is to be placed "underground" three of the holes can be omitted.

Description

The nest box consists of what looks like a large flower pot turned upside down and fitted on to a circular concrete base. To let the bees into the nest box, the flower pot has holes cut into it, all of which at ground level will coincide with holes cast into the base. The base, which has a central drainage hole, gives the box good stability.

The holes in the bottom of the flower pot (which is the top of the box) provide vital ventilation and are covered with net to keep out the vermin. To protect it from the rain, the top of the box is covered by an umbrella made from a plastic bottle. The finished box can be covered with vegetation to disguise its shiny surface and square shape.

The four entrances heighten the chance of a queen bumble bee finding the nest. Once a bee is settled inside, the superfluous holes can be blocked off and the design offers easy ways of doing this.

Materials For One Completed Nest Box With Four Entrances

For The Nest Box

2 identical flower pots of about 10 litre (18 pints) capacity, e.g. Sankey or Soparco
Diameter of top: about 280mm (11 inches)
Height: about 230mm (9 inches)
1 small 60mm (2½inch) flower pot or something similar

A length of 22mm (0.9 inch) rigid plastic pipe (plumbing). 200 mm (8inches) is needed
1 22mm (0.9 inch) copper connector with 90° bend
2 x 15mm (½inch) No. 6 screws (or similar) with suitable plastic plugs
Sand, e.g. builders' sand
Concrete mix with fine aggregate (In addition to the sand; or can be bought ready-mixed)
Galvinised chicken wire, 13mm (½ inch) mesh preferred (concrete reinforcement and basket for nest)
A roll of kitchen paper towels
A roll of plastic "cling" film
Polyester net, e.g. net curtain material fine enough and strong enough to keep out ants
Moss, dead bracken or similar (to disguise the nest box and umbrella)
A proprietary all purpose adhesive

For The Umbrella

A tall 2 litre or 1.5 litre (4 or 3 pint) plastic drinks bottle
A cork, a 50mm (2 inches) No. 6 screw and a small piece of wood (see assembly instructions)

To Set Up The Nest

Nest material (see Chapter 4)
Feeder Version 2 (see Chapter 5)
(Galvinised chicken wire)

To Make The Concrete Base

1. Cut three holes in the side of one of the large flowerpots spacing them evenly round the pot and avoiding any reinforcing struts. Two of the holes should be about 30mm (1¼ inch) diameter with their bottom edges about 50mm (2 inches) from the top. The third hole should be about 25mm (1 inch) diameter with its bottom edge about 15mm (½ inch) from the top (see diagram). This is best done by marking where the hole will be with a labelling pen, making several small holes in its middle with a bradawl or screwdriver and enlarging them with a sharp knife with a narrow blade.

2. Avoiding these holes, drill two small holes opposite one another about 20mm (¾ inch) from the top of the pot.

3. Smear the inside of the top of the pot in a band about 25mm (1 inch) wide with a little grease, e.g. vaseline, margarine. With the aim of preventing the concrete sticking to the pot, hang strips of cling film round it's inside pressing them onto the greasy surface so that there are few wrinkles. (See diagram)

4. From the outside screw a 15mm screw through each of the two small holes, the cling film and a little way into a plastic plug on the inside. Make sure the plug is touching the pot side. (See diagram)

5. After roughly covering the drainage holes in the bottom of the pot with newspaper, fill it with sand up to the bottom lip of the larger holes, shaking the sand down to the bottom lip of the larger holes, shake well to make sure the sand is solidly packed.

6. Cut crosses in the cling film covering the holes. Now make two wads of kitchen towel which will fill the two larger holes and protrude into the pot about 40mm (1½ inches). It helps to wrap them round a stick. Cover them with cling film an place them in the holes. (See diagram)

7. Cut two pieces of 22mm (0.9 inch) plastic pipe about 100mm (4 inches) long. Push the end of one piece into a square of cling film and then into the copper connector. Smooth the film up the length of pipe. Repeat the operation with the other piece of pipe to make an L-shape. From the inside of the pot, push one end of the assembly a short way through the small hole and then press the other free end onto the sand. The pipe coming through the hole must be kept horizontal. (See diagram)

8. Add more sand to the pot so that it comes halfway up each large hole. At the same time there must be about 25mm (1 inch) clearance between the horizontal pipe and the sand beneath it. Shape the surface of the sand so that it slopes up very slightly to the middle. Once again shake the sand down hard.

9. From wood about 10mm (½ inch) thick, cut a square about 5mm (¼ inch) bigger than the diameter of the feeder that will be placed in the nest. Set it horizontal on the sand and hard up

against the side halfway between two holes and not near a screw.

10. Now cover the sand base with cling film.

NEST BOX 1

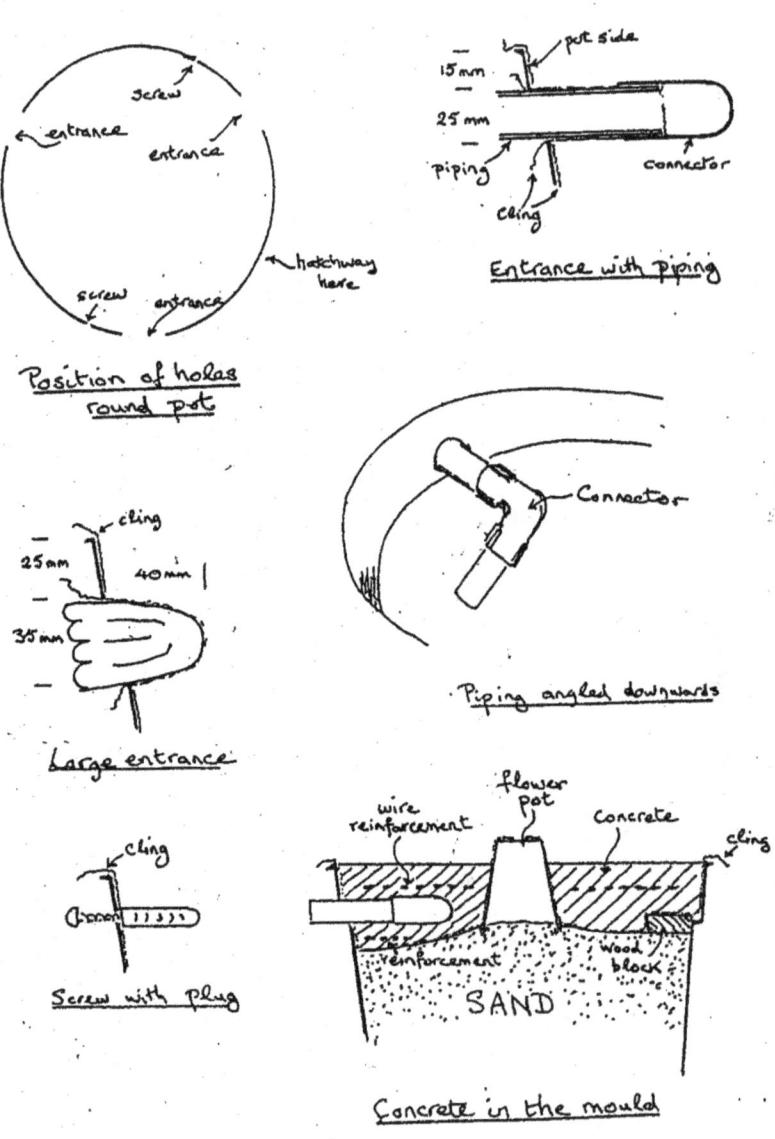

11. Cover the outside of the small flower pot with cling film and press it open end down into the middle of the sand base. Its top should be well above the lip of the big flower pot. (See diagram) The mould for the base of the nest box is complete.

12. Cut some chicken wire (reinforcement) to make a piece 600 x 100mm (24 x 4 inches) and form it into a ring that will fit in the mould without touching the sides or sticking out of the concrete when in place. Cut one more small piece of wire about 100 x 50mm (4 x 2 inches) that will fit under the pipe to reinforce this vulnerable point.

13. Mix enough concrete to fill the mould. The mixture should be rather wet. Fill the mould a little at a time, starting with the edges. Make sure that the mix runs under the pipe and then insert the small piece of wire. Continue filling until the bottom is covered and then place the ring of wire in the mould and continue filling. During the process shake the concrete down repeatedly by lifting the pot up a little and dropping it onto a hard surface. Finish with a flat top and allow to set. (See diagram)

14. When dry, remove the screws, piping and paper wads from the outside. Then remove the concrete base from its mould, knock out the centre pot, pull out the piping and the piece of wood, and clear away any shrink film. Wash the base and clear out the tunnel, making sure the plastic tubing will fit nicely into it from the outside. Make sure there is no obstruction between the *feeder recess*, made by the wood insert, and the side of the pot. Empty the flower pot of everything, wash it and check that it fits the base.

Completing the Nest Box

1. Take the large flower pot that was used to mould the concrete base and draw a line round its body close to the bottom with a labelling pen, avoiding any hole. (See diagram) With a sharp knife, cut round the pot, following the line, to make an open-ended cylinder. Sand paper the edge. Fit this cylinder onto the concrete base to make the *nest box body* and loosely fit it in place with the screws.

2. From the inside of the *body*, make two small holes through its side to mark the bottom corners of the *feeder recess*. Now take

the body apart again and, using the holes as reference, cut the pot to make the **feeder hatch**. (See diagram) This should be on the same level as the **recess** when opened but slightly wider. The side cuts should be about 40mm (1½ inches) long. Reassemble and make sure the **hatch** opens enough to get the feeder in and out and then clicks shut.

3. Take the second large pot and cut round it in a similar way (see 1. above) but this time about 140mm (5½inches) from the bottom. (See diagram) This shortened pot will fit tightly over the **nest box body** to make the removable **nest box top**. Make sure it does not interfere with the **feeder hatch**.

4. On the side of the **top** and about 25mm (1 inch) from the edge, draw a circle about 40mm (1½ inches) diameter and cut it out. Placing the **top** on the **body**, mark an equivalent circle in its side through the hole and cut it out to make a matching hole. This makes the fourth entrance into the nest when the two holes are lined up.

5. Take the **nest box top** and make sure there are enough large holes in its roof to provide good ventilation. If necessary enlarge them or add to them. Now drill a small hole through the middle of the roof. Cut a circle of polyester net large enough to cover the surface of the roof and hang down the sides far enough to cover any other holes. Make a small hole in its centre. Put a screw through this hole and temporarily fix it to the roof of the nest box. Run a bead of adhesive round the **nest box top** and stick the net to it so that ants etc. cannot get underneath and so gain entry to the nest. Trim the net when the glue is dry. (See diagram)

6. Cut off the top and bottom of the drinks bottle to make a cylinder at least 230mm (9 inches) long. Slit up the cylinder and drill a small hole in the centre of the plastic sheet that results. This will be the umbrella to prevent rain getting into the nest. Drill a hole end to end through the cork which may need to be shortened. Put the long screw through roof, net, cork and umbrella and screw it into the piece of wood to make the assembly tight. (See diagram.) Trim round the plastic umbrella. The piece of wood becomes the handle for the removable **nest box top** which is now complete.

NEST BOX 1

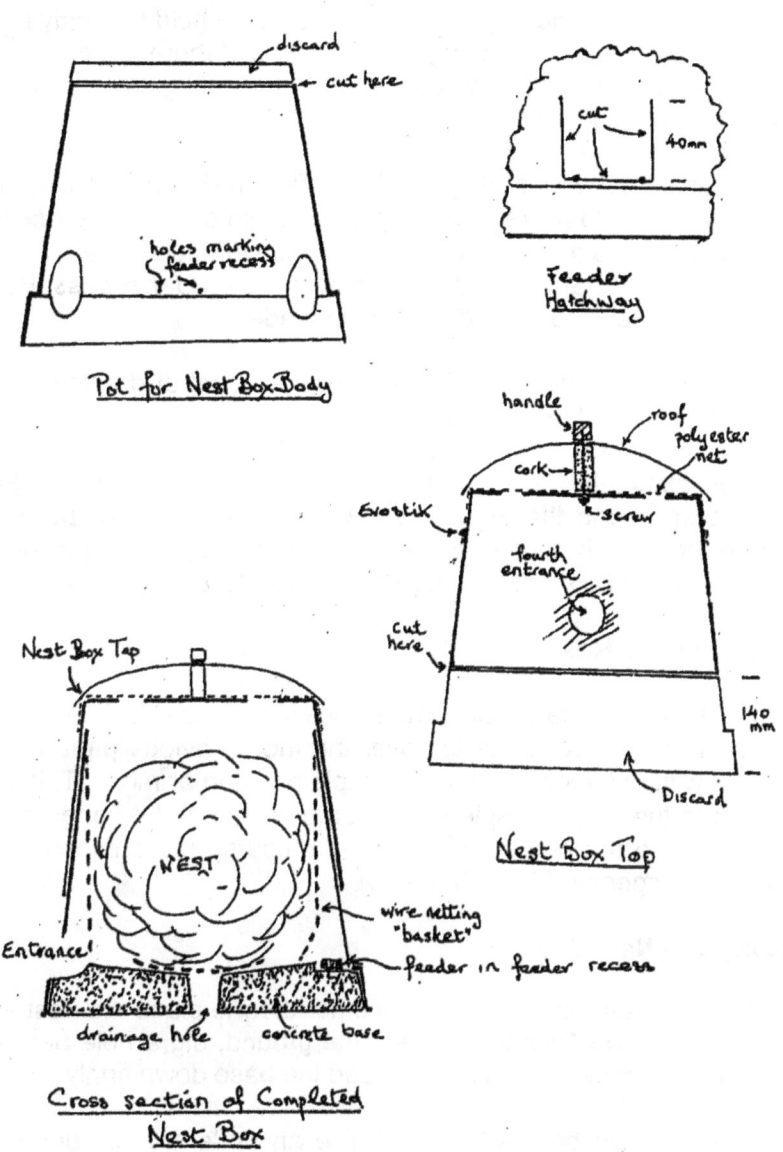

Assembly

1. Assemble the **nest box body**, lining up the holes in its various parts and screwing in the fixing screws which hold the body to its base. Make sure everything fits and works. If there are any holes visible from the inside through which ants could gain entry, block them with wood filler or something similar.

2. Cut a piece of wire netting to 150 x 700mm (6 x 28 inches) and join the ends to make a cylinder. Drop it into the **nest box body**. This will contain the nest material but leave space at the edges for ventilation. Shape it round and over the **feeder recess**. Bees will easily get through the wire to the feeder.

3. Cut another piece of netting to cover the central drainage hole and to support the nest material.

4. Later, complete the nest box by adding the nest material (See Chapter 4) and the feeder (See Chapter 5). This can be done when the box has been placed at its permanent site. The feeder is put in and taken out through the **feeder hatch**. (See diagram)

Disguising The Nest

In Chapter 6 it was said that bumble bees look for a nest that is well-used so it is an advantage to cover the more obvious parts of the nest box with old vegetation, for example bracken or moss. This can be stuck to the box or stapled to the umbrella so that it hangs down and breaks up the regular shape. It is of course more important to disguise the opening (See Chapter 6).

Placing The Nest Box

There is little that needs to be done other than to place the nest at a suitable site. (See Chapter 6) Clear the ground, dig a hole beneath where the drainage hole will be and bed the base down firmly.

One opening can be made to look like an underground tunnel by inserting a piece of piping in it and covering it with turf. (See Chapter 3: An underground nest.)

When a bee occupies the nest it will only use one of the entrances. The others should therefore be blocked off. To block off a hole in the base, shape a small piece of foam, e.g. from a kitchen sponge, and push it well into the hole. This will provide ventilation but keep out vermin. To close the upper hole, simply twist the *top* on the *body*.

As the nest grows in size it may be necessary to increase the ventilation to avoid condensation. This can easily be done by either:
1) Lifting the nest up and slipping two strips of wood underneath. Do this in the evening when the bees are home to avoid confusing them.
2) Burrowing under the base with a trowel to make a tunnel to the drainage hole.

Variation For An Underground Nest

This variation, whose only entrance is through a tunnel, is designed for burying reasonably deep in the ground – in a rockery for example. Good ventilation is provided by underground tubing which comes up beneath the central drainage hole (See Chapter 3).

Extra Materials

Plastic tubing to make the underground ventilation duct, e.g. flexible vacuum cleaner tubing.

Variation In Design

1. Cut only one hole in the flower pot for the *nest box body*, the one that takes the plastic piping.

2. Make the concrete base with one entrance for the plastic piping. Make sure the central drainage hole will be big enough to receive the plastic ventilation tubing.

3. The nest box top should be made much shorter and there must be no entrance holes cut in it. Cut the top so that it overlaps the body by at least 75mm (3inches). this allows the body to be buried deeply if that is really necessary and the top, which is above ground, to be removed easily as well.

Placing The Nest Box

Choose a site on a gentle bank if you can. Dig a hole big enough for the modified nest box so that the earth will cover the entrance into it and the tubing leading from it. Dig a shallow trench away from the hole having chosen the length to suit your needs ant that of the surrounding ground. Place the ***nest box*** in the hole with its opening at the front of the bank Insert a piece of plastic tubing into the hole in the nest box. It should slope up into the nest if possible. Push the tubing home firmly. Now fill in the trench until the tubing is hidden and disguised. Make its opening inviting by enlarging it and scratching the ground leading to it to simulate a mouse run. If the piping slopes down into the box it may fill with water so drill small drainage holes in it where necessary.

Other Variations

The basic design can be used to make smaller nest boxes but these will only be suitable for the bees that make smaller colonies.

Nest Box Design 2

This is a small nest box which is placed on the ground. It will cater for the smaller surface-nesting bees but may also be used by those needing larger premises. It basically consists of two flower pots fixed together mouth to mouth.

Materials

For The Nest Box

2 flower pots, 200mm (8 inches) diameter, e.g. Optipot 4 litre
4 small screws, e.g. 12mm (½ inch) No. 6
Polyester net curtain material
Small piece of wood
1 empty plastic bottle, 1.5litre or 21litre size
Adhesive

For The Nest

Nest material (See Chapter 4)
Feeder version 1 (See Chapter 5)
A piece of galvinised chicken wire 13mm mesh (½ inch), about 15 x 20cms (6 x 8inches)
Stones or gravel

Making The Nest Box

On the same flowerpot:
1. a) Cut off the bottom: trace a line round the pot with a marker about 25mm (1inch) above the bottom and cut with a sharp knife following this line. (See diagram)
   b) Cut off the top: trace a line round the pot about half way between the top and the shoulder and cut following the line. (See diagram)

2. Cut three notches each about 25mm (1 inch) apart in the edge of the top of this pot. Mark where they are with a bit of Sellotape – office sticky tape stuck to the side below. This will be the bottom of the nest box.

3. Fit this cut flowerpot inside the other one. (See diagram) Make sure it fits in well without gaps but also without too much distortion. If necessary cut a little more off the pot.

4. Now bore three holes in the top of the untouched flower pot. The holes should be equidistant from each other and just beneath the rim. Make them large enough for the screws and clear them of all debris.

5. Fit the first pot snugly into the other with the marked "bottom" midway between two screw holes. Set the pots upright and adjust the position of the one inside the other until the assembly is square and the inner pot is truly round. Bow bore two holes in the inner pot that correspond to the three in the outer pot and fix the two together with screws. (See diagram)

6. Set the assembly upright with the closed end at the top. Cut out two circles of polyester net that will cover the holes in the bottom and sides of the pot with some over. Sandpaper the surface of the pot in a ring round the pot below any holes and then apply adhesive to fix it firmly. Trim when the glue is dry. This protects the nest from ants. (See diagram)

7. Take the bottom that was cut off the first pot and enlarge one of the holes in it to about 25mm (1 inch) diameter or a little larger. Now bore a small hole in its centre, bore a hole in the piece of wood and make a small hole in the centre of the second polyester net circle. Fix the three together with a screw through

the holes according to the diagram. Glue the polyester net down as above and, when dry, cut the excess back to the cut edge of the flowerpot bottom. When this assembly is fitted like a cork into the open end of the other part of the nest box, it becomes the "door". Cut a hole in the net to correspond with the enlarged hole in the door. This will be the entrance to the nest at the *bottom* of the door.

8. Clear any labels from the old drinks bottle which should be clean. Cut a straight line lengthways up the bottle and then cut two circular sections from it, each about 50mm (2inches) deep. These will become "overhangs" for the two ends of the nest box to prevent rain getting into the nest. Sandpaper a 25mm (1inch) strip along the inside of one edge of both sections and apply adhesive to them. Apply a bead of adhesive to the net on the *top* of the box and the *top* of the door. Stick one section to each position to make the overhangs. (See diagram) When dry, trim them with scissors. The door should fit snugly into the box to make a good seal.

Setting Up The Nest

1. Make sure that water will drain out of the bottom of the nest box through the slots in it. If necessary, wedge one or two matchsticks between the two layers.

2. Having chosen the site, cut a shallow trench in the ground and dig a drainage hole at its centre. Put stones or gravel in the bottom of the nest box to weigh it down so that it will sit firmly in place without being blown away or dislodged. Set the nest box in place.

3. Make the piece of chicken wire into a shallow boat and see that it will fit into the nest box, resting easily on the stones but also with plenty of air beneath it and around it. Make the nest material into an oblong ball, place it on the wire base and push it all well into the box. Make sure the nest material is clear of the end. Place the feeder just inside the door and fit the door. (See diagram)

NEST BOX 2

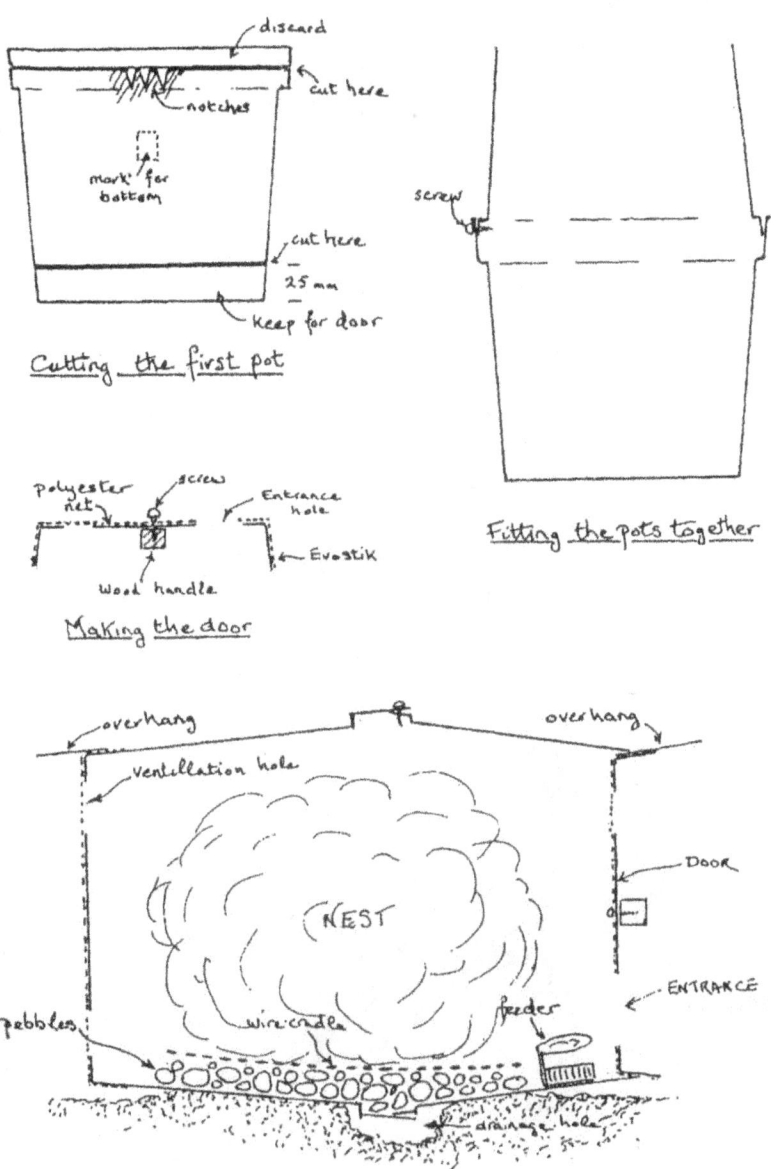

The completed nest in place

www.ingramcontent.com/pod-product-compliance
Lightning Source LLC
Chambersburg PA
CBHW080416170426
43194CB00015B/2831